LIVING EACH DAY WITH JESUS

Inspiration and Guidance for Daily Living

A *Jesus in My Pocket* Book

You shall love the LORD your God
with all your heart,
with all your soul, and with all your mind.

Matthew 22:37

Thomas Nelson Publishers
Nashville

Living Each Day with Jesus
Inspiration and Guidance for Daily Living
A *Jesus in My Pocket* Book

Jesus in My Pocket Ministries
PMB #327
6632 Telegraph Road
Bloomfield, MI 48301

Printed in Mexico
1 2 3 4 5 6 . . . 04 03 02 01 00 99

Just for today...

I will honor the Lord with gratitude before I rise. I will give thanks for the morning sun and for the gift of life. Before I place my feet on the floor, I will remember that whatever I am called to today, I am doing the Lord's work. In Jesus' name I will rise and greet the new day.

God's Word says...

This is the day the LORD has made;
We will rejoice and be glad in it.

Psalm 118:24

Just for You

Jesus in My Pocket

Fold Here

FROM: ____________________

TO: ____________________

____

Just for today...

I will exercise charity in all I do, in all I say, and even in my thoughts. I will remember that every person is a creation of God, and I will be charitable to them in any way I can—by sharing a smile, a kind word, a helping hand, or a gift of love. I will do these things with a loving heart as Jesus has commanded.

God's Word says...

Beloved, let us love one another, for love is of God; and everyone who loves is born of God and knows God.

1 John 4:7

Jesus in My Pocket

Just for You

Fold Here

FROM: ____________________

TO: ____________________

____

Just for today...

I will thank Jesus for this new day and for opening my eyes to experience the gift of life. I will pray for His guidance in all I do today. I will not get out of bed until I have promised Him that I won't start the day by complaining or bemoaning my fate. Instead, I will trust in His promises and know that He loves me.

God's Word says...

You will show me the path of life;
In Your presence is fullness of joy;
At Your right hand are pleasures
forevermore.

Psalm 16:11

Jesus in My Pocket

Just for You

Fold Here

FROM: ____________________

TO: ____________________

____

Just for today...

I will be kind to those less fortunate than me. I will not look down on them or blame them for their circumstances. Instead, I will be kind and offer my sympathy, even if silently, knowing that kindness is another expression of love. I will remember that Jesus asked us not to judge one another.

God´s Word says...

Judge not, that you be not judged. For with what judgment you judge, you will be judged; and with the measure you use, it will be measured back to you.

Matthew 7:1-2

Jesus in My Pocket

Just for You

Fold Here

FROM: ______________________

TO: ______________________

____

Just for today...

I will practice forgiveness. I will forgive the driver who tailgates me, the shopper who cuts line in front of me, the rude teller at the bank. I will forgive my coworkers who gossip about me, and those who have cheated me. I will forgive them as Jesus forgives me for the wrongs I do.

God's Word says...

Bearing with one another, and forgiving one another, if anyone has a complaint against another; even as Christ forgave you, so you also must do.

Colossians 3:13

Just for You

Jesus in My Pocket

Fold Here

FROM: ____________________

TO: ____________________

____

Just for today...

I will stop whatever I am doing at least once and softly speak Jesus' name. I will close my eyes and let His presence fill me. I will remember that no matter what I am doing, or how I am feeling, Jesus is always with me. Whispering His name will remind me of His eternal vigilance over me.

God's Word says...

Whoever confesses that Jesus is the Son of God, God abides in him, and he in God. And we have known and believed the love that God has for us.

1 John 4:15-16

Jesus in My Pocket

Just for You

Fold Here

FROM: ____________

TO: ____________

____

Just for today...

I will not covet my neighbor's goods. I will not long for the bigger house, the newer car, or the finer jewelry. I will thank Jesus for what He has provided for me, and know that envying another's possessions does not bring me closer to the Lord.

God's Word says...

And He said to them, "Take heed and beware of covetousness, for one's life does not consist in the abundance of the things he possesses."

Luke 12:15

Just for You

Jesus in My Pocket

Fold Here

FROM: ____________________

TO: ____________________

____

Just for today...

I will rest when I get tired and not push myself to do one more thing. While I am resting, I will take the time to thank the Lord for giving me such a full life—that there is always something to be done. I will remember that taking a break with Jesus is the best way to spend my time after all.

God's Word says...

To everything there is a season,
A time for every purpose under heaven.

Ecclesiastes 3:1

Just for You

Jesus in My Pocket

Fold Here

FROM: ____________________

TO: ____________________

____

Just for today...

I will remember to pray—not just to call for help or ask for favors, but to offer prayers of gratitude, for in my heart I am thankful for so many things. I will think about my blessings, no matter how small they may seem. I will thank and praise Jesus for those blessings and not ask for anything—just for today.

God's Word says...

Giving thanks always for all things to God the Father in the name of our Lord Jesus Christ.

Ephesians 5:20

Jesus in My Pocket

Just for You

Fold Here

FROM: ____________________

TO: ____________________

____

Just for today...

I will find one small way to simplify my life. By having less to worry about, I will have more room for Jesus. Instead of being busy every minute, I will eliminate one task or one errand, and spend that time, instead, focusing on Jesus.

God's Word says...

Therefore I say to you, do not worry about your life, what you will eat or what you will drink; nor about your body, what you will put on. Is not life more than food and the body more than clothing?

Matthew 6:25

Just for You

Jesus in My Pocket

Fold Here

FROM: ____________________

TO: ____________________

____

Just for today...

I will find beauty in an otherwise overlooked object—like my empty laundry basket, a clean bathroom floor, a well-prepared meal. Just as the Sistine chapel was painted, or the Eifel tower built, so too are the tasks of my day objects of beauty, performed with love for those for whom I care.

God's Word says...

As each one has received a gift, minister it to one another, as good stewards of the manifold grace of God. . . . If anyone ministers, let him do it as with the ability which God supplies, that in all things God may be glorified through Jesus Christ.

1 Peter 4:10-11

Jesus in My Pocket

Just for You

Fold Here

FROM: ____________________

TO: ____________________

____

Just for today...

I will let go of one heartbreak. I will stop agonizing over whatever it is that has made me unhappy and turn it over to the Lord. I will stop remembering every detail, every injustice—recalling every painful word—and, instead, I will offer it all up to the Lord and let it go.

God's Word says...

Why are you cast down, O my soul?
And why are you disquieted within me?
Hope in God, for I shall yet praise Him
For the help of His countenance.

Psalm 42:5

Jesus in My Pocket

Just for You

Fold Here

FROM: ______________

TO: ______________

____

Just for today...

I will stop whatever I am doing and take the time to appreciate nature. I will look closely at the lilac bush, the robin in the tree, the snow on the ground or the cactus on my windowsill. I will marvel at the perfection in every leaf, every feather, every snowflake, and know that I am seeing the handiwork of God.

God's Word says...

God saw everything that He had made, and indeed it was very good.

Genesis 1:31

Jesus in My Pocket

Just for You

Fold Here

FROM: ____________________

TO: ____________________

____

Just for today...

I will remember to honor my loved ones. I will forget their flaws and focus, instead, on the things I love about them—their sense of humor, their curly hair, the way they always wear their shoelaces untied.

God's Word says...

Therefore let us pursue the things which make for peace and the things by which one may edify another.

Romans 14:19

Just for You

Jesus in My Pocket

Fold Here

FROM: ____________

TO: ____________

____

Just for today...

I will look at children with a sense of awe. I will see their games as their work, hear their cries as their souls' longing, and smell their freshness as the breath of the Lord. I will also remember the child in me, and give myself freedom to play, to cry, and to rejoice in God.

God's Word says...

Jesus said, "Let the little children come to Me, and do not forbid them; for of such is the kingdom of heaven."

Matthew 19:14

Jesus in My Pocket

Just for You

Fold Here

FROM: ____________________

TO: ____________________

____

Just for today...

I will thank Jesus for the work I have to do, even if it is work I don't always enjoy. I will find some positive aspect of my work to dwell on, while I remember that my true work on earth is to honor the Lord and to abide by His commandments.

God's Word says...

Fear God and keep His commandments,
For this is man's all.
For God will bring every work into
judgment,
Including every secret thing,
Whether good or evil.

Ecclesiastes 12:13

Just for You

Jesus in My Pocket

Fold Here

FROM: ______________

TO: ______________

____

Just for today...

I will not steal. I will not try to see how much I can get away with at work, or what I can pull over on my neighbor or my government. I will not try to justify myself by claiming "they owe it to me." Instead, I will act with integrity and know that whatever I take that is not mine is stealing.

God's Word says...

No temptation has overtaken you except such as is common to man; but God is faithful, who will not allow you to be tempted beyond what you are able, but with the temptation will also make the way of escape, that you may be able to bear it.

1 Corinthians 10:13

Just for You

Jesus in My Pocket

Fold Here

FROM: ____________________

TO: ____________________

____

Just for today...

No matter where I work—the office, the hospital, the factory or my home—I will keep Jesus' name on my lips, in my thoughts, in my words and in my deeds. I know that He will be with me, that the promises of His Word will guide me, and that contentment and happiness in my work will be pleasing to the Lord.

God's Word says...

And whatever you do, do it heartily, as to the Lord and not to men.

Colossians 3:23

Jesus in My Pocket

Just for You

Fold Here

FROM: ____________________

TO: ____________________

____

Just for today...

I will remember to give thanks to God before I eat my meals. Having been blessed with the gift of food, I will thank Jesus with all my heart for His goodness and for His promise to give us each day our daily bread.

God's Word says...

Therefore by Him let us continually offer the sacrifice of praise to God, that is, the fruit of our lips, giving thanks to His name.

Hebrews 13:15

Jesus in My Pocket

Just for You

Fold Here

FROM: ____________________

TO: ____________________

____

Just for today...

I will accept as fact that Jesus loves me. I will not covet the love relationships of other people, or question why I haven't found the "love of my life," but I will remember, instead, that the most precious love of Jesus is my salvation. Then I will thank Him for loving me and for sending human love my way in His time.

God's Word says...

For God so loved the world that He gave His only begotten Son, that whoever believes in Him should not perish but have everlasting life.

John 3:16

Jesus in My Pocket

Just for You

Fold Here

FROM: ____________________

TO: ____________________

____

Just for today...

I will be humble before God and others. I will say "thank you" when someone compliments me, and I will make it a point to compliment someone else in return. I will keep in mind that humility is a gift of self-acceptance from the Lord.

God's Word says...

Everyone who exalts himself will be humbled, and he who humbles himself will be exalted.

Luke 18:14

Jesus in My Pocket

Just for You

Fold Here

FROM: ____________________

TO: ____________________

____

Just for today...

I will persevere. No matter what my circumstances or personal challenges may be, I will thank God for giving me the opportunity to serve Him in all I do, in all I face, and I will live my life one day at a time.

God's Word says...

Therefore do not cast away your confidence, which has great reward. For you have need of endurance, so that after you have done the will of God, you may receive the promise.

Hebrews 10:35-36

Just for You

Jesus in My Pocket

Fold Here

FROM: ____________________

TO: ____________________

____

Just for today...

I will stop feeling sorry for myself. No matter how low I feel, I will put on a happy face and remind myself—as often as I need to—that Jesus loves me, that it is always darkest just before the dawn, and that my depression will eventually pass.

God's Word says...

Hope deferred makes the heart sick,
But when the desire comes, it is a tree of life.

Proverbs 13:12

Just for You

Jesus in My Pocket

Fold Here

FROM: ____________________

TO: ____________________

____

Just for today...

I will reach out to someone in need. Whether that means I will make a phone call, offer my time, or prepare a meal, I will find some way to let another person know that I care about them. By doing so I will be passing along the love that Jesus gives to me every day.

God's Word says...

Let each of you look out not only for his own interests, but also for the interests of others.

Philippians 2:4

Jesus in My Pocket

Just for You

Fold Here

FROM: ____________

TO: ____________

____

Just for today...

I will not worry about my debts. Fear and worry will not produce positive results; instead, they only produce more fear and worry. I will take the steps made possible to me through the Lord Jesus to provide for my needs, release my anxiety, and thank Him for seeing me through the lean times.

God's Word says...

These things I have spoken to you, that in Me you may have peace. In the world you will have tribulation; but be of good cheer, I have overcome the world.

John 16:33

Just for You

Jesus in My Pocket

Fold Here

FROM: ____________

TO: ____________

____

Just for today...

I will act honestly in all my dealings with others. Whether I am offering a service, a product, or an opinion, I will not speak falsely, but I will be honest and forthright, and not stretch the truth to suit my purpose.

God's Word says...

Therefore, putting away lying, "Let each one of you speak truth with his neighbor," for we are members of one another.

Ephesians 4:25

Jesus in My Pocket

Just for You

Fold Here

FROM: ______________

TO: ______________

____

Just for today...

I will listen to others with compassion. I will try to hear the emotion behind their words and remember that we all act out of love or fear. I will try to empathize with the person who is entrusting their feelings to me, and silently ask God for guidance. I will remember that I do not need to solve anyone's problems.

God's Word says...

Bear one another's burdens, and so fulfill the law of Christ. For if anyone thinks himself to be something, when he is nothing, he deceives himself.

Galatians 6:2-3

Jesus in My Pocket

Just for You

Fold Here

FROM: ____________________

TO: ____________________

____

Just for today...

I will sing to the Lord. Even if I cannot carry a tune, or I sing off-key, I will sing to Him from my heart with gladness and joy. I will offer my song to Jesus and know that it is a sweet sound in His ear.

God's Word says...

The Lord is my strength and my shield;
My heart trusted in Him, and I am
helped;
Therefore my heart greatly rejoices,
And with my song I will praise Him.

Psalm 28:7

Just for You

Jesus in My Pocket

Fold Here

FROM: ____________________

TO: ____________________

____

Just for today...

I will pray—not only before I go to sleep, but whenever the Spirit impresses me, I will begin talking directly to God. Prayer is the longing of my heart, spoken to God in the same way I would speak to my best friend. I will remember that the perfect prayer expresses gratitude, so I will thank God first of all for listening to me.

God's Word says...

Hear my cry, O God;
Attend to my prayer.
From the end of the earth I will cry to You,
When my heart is overwhelmed;
Lead me to the rock that is higher than I.

Psalm 61:1-2

Jesus in My Pocket

Just for You

Fold Here

FROM: ____________________

TO: ____________________

____

Just for today...

I will read my Bible instead of the newspaper. Instead of filling my mind with what is ungodly in this world, I will fill myself with the good news from God's Word. I will spend time reflecting on His message, and learn how His promises will make my life better.

God's Word says...

Therefore you shall lay up these words of mine in your heart and in your soul, and bind them as a sign on your hand, and they shall be as frontlets between your eyes.

Deuteronomy 11:18

Jesus in My Pocket

Just for You

Fold Here

FROM: ____________

TO: ____________

____

Just for today...

I will rest and trust in the Lord. Without expecting all of my problems to be solved overnight, I will stop thinking about them for today and focus my attention on the bounty and love that comes from the Lord Jesus.

God's Word says...

Now faith is the substance of things hoped for, the evidence of things not seen. . . . But without faith it is impossible to please Him, for he who comes to God must believe that He is, and that He is a rewarder of those who diligently seek Him.

Hebrews 11:1, 6

To accept Jesus Christ as your personal Lord and Savior, pray out loud:

Heavenly Father,
I come to You in the name of Jesus. I believe in my heart that Jesus Christ is the Son of God, that He died on the Cross for my sins and was raised from the dead for my justification. I believe in my heart, and I now confess with my mouth that Jesus is Lord. Therefore, I am saved!